Afterthoughts

Afterthoughts

Poems to Heal the Heart
for Adolescents and Their Parents and Guardians

"Trust thyself; every heart vibrates to that iron string."
—Ralph Waldo Emerson

iUniverse, Inc.
Bloomington

Afterthoughts
Poems to Heal the Heart for Adolescents and Their Parents and Guardians

iUniverse books may be ordered through booksellers or by contacting:

iUniverse
1663 Liberty Drive
Bloomington, IN 47403
www.iuniverse.com
1-800-Authors (1-800-288-4677)

Because of the dynamic nature of the Internet, any web addresses or links contained in this book may have changed since publication and may no longer be valid. The views expressed in this work are solely those of the author and do not necessarily reflect the views of the publisher, and the publisher hereby disclaims any responsibility for them.

Any people depicted in stock imagery provided by Thinkstock are models, and such images are being used for illustrative purposes only.

Certain stock imagery © Thinkstock.

ISBN: 978-1-4620-1463-7 (sc)
ISBN: 978-1-4620-1464-4 (ebk)

Printed in the United States of America

iUniverse rev. date: 08/15/2011

Afterthoughts

Poems to Heal the Heart
for Adolescents and Their Parents/Guardians

Written by Mrs. D.
Illustrated by Tara Balboa

iUniverse®
©*Ann Dinicola 6/07/07*

addiction, adolescence, anxiety, death, divorce, drugs, fear, future, hope, illness, love, parents, relationships, respect, self, suicide, abuse, academics,

In counseling, I have found
that very often the written word
has a greater impact than the spoken word.

Enclosed within the circle are the various topics discussed in Afterthoughts.
They are extremely serious issues that many adolescents and their parents/guardians face each and every day.
Knowing that someone else has shared the same pain often helps to heal an aching heart.

The writings that follow will stir different emotions within different people; therefore,
I have created several blank pages titled "My Afterthoughts"
that will allow you to share your most private thoughts.
Please take the time to read, reflect and write what you are feeling.

With love,
Mrs. D.

To a very special someone
who was afraid
to stop and smell the roses.

"When the world says, 'Give up,' hope whispers, 'Try it one more time.'"
—Anonymous

Contents

Acknowledgments

Afterthoughts is a journey into the world of adolescence as seen through the eyes of a high school counselor. Each and every day a very special someone meanders into my office knowing that it is a safe haven in which to bare his/her soul. It is behind closed doors that tears fall, heartfelt stories unfold, and answers to life's most difficult questions begin to surface. It is with sincere gratitude that I say thank you to all those beautiful young people and their parents/guardians who have trusted me with their deepest thoughts. In return, I share with you my response in poetry and prose to their precious words, along with "My Afterthoughts," a journal created especially for you … your hopes … your dreams. The written word is a powerful tool for healing. Please listen to your inner voice and know that you are never alone. You are that special someone who is in the throes of adolescence; you will survive; the sun will shine tomorrow if only you believe in you!

Listen to Your Heart … Your Inner Voice

As this young girl searches for answers to life's most difficult questions, she feels overwhelmed … and then she hears a voice.

Heart
Only five letters
Two vowels
Three consonants
One syllable

The main organ
Keeps one alive
One beat at a time
Uninterrupted

Look inside … he*ar*t
Three letters
Two vowels
One syllable … *ear*

Listen to your he*ar*t
H*ear* the voice
Whose voice … your voice
H*ear* what your he*ar*t is saying

I'm scared
F*ear* consumes … he*ar*t races
A gentle t*ear* falls
Help me

I am always n*ear*
Day after day, y*ear* after y*ear*
H*ear* me
Do not f*ear* me

Feel me beating
H*ear* my thoughts
Se*ar*ch deep inside
Dear heart … I hear you.

11

My Afterthoughts

Date: _____

_____
_____
_____
_____
_____
_____
_____
_____
_____
_____
_____
_____
_____
_____
_____
_____
_____
_____
_____

The Me I Need to Be

One bright sunny morning a very confused seventeen-year-old boy appeared at my office door. A look of despair was on his face. He asked if he could speak with me.

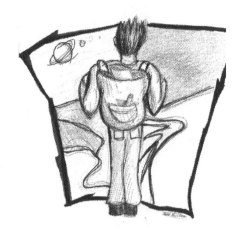

As he spoke, his eyes stayed fixed on the floor. Every once in a while he was able to look at me. His words were similar to those I've heard several times before: "My mother and I had a fight this morning." But as he spoke his leg began to shake, and his voice began to quiver. Yet he continued to speak of the past two years and how upset he was that he and his mother could no longer speak without fighting. He was tired of all the fighting. He wanted it to stop. He wanted to tell her how he really felt. He wanted to let her know what his opinion of life was. He wanted to let her know that he wanted to have fun. He wanted to let her to know that he was tired of getting good grades. He wanted to let her to know that money wasn't important to him. He wanted to let her know that being happy was more important than money. He wanted to let her know that his friend's suicide changed his life … but he couldn't. He didn't know that he was so affected by her death that it changed the course of his life. He didn't know that he was in the midst of grieving a life that was taken so quickly. He didn't know that he was in the midst of growing up … questioning all that he was taught … searching for his own self … searching for the meaning of life … searching for his own independence.

He did learn today that there are some things in life that are out of our control. He did learn today that he is in control of his life. He did learn today that life is a series of choices. He did learn today that he has chosen life. He did learn today that he is responsible for the choices he makes for himself. He did learn today that he loves his parents immensely. He did learn today that his parents are people, people with opinions. He did learn today that he has a right to have his own opinions. He did learn today that he is growing up. He did learn today that he is in the throes of becoming independent. He did learn today that he is becoming a man … a man who wants to be happy … a man who wants to be able to balance fun and work … a man who wants to be able to have time to play with his kids … a man who is searching for the meaning of life … a man who is becoming the *me* he needs to be. His journey has begun.

My Afterthoughts

_____

_____

_____

_____

_____

_____

_____

_____

_____

_____

_____

_____

_____

_____

_____

_____

Not Like All the Others

Today a young boy walked into my office, a freshman. He sat down. He spoke. His words were deep. He was living with alcoholic parents. He is surviving ... one day at a time.

He is only fourteen years old.
His clothes look like all the others.
His voice sounds like all the others.
His heart beats like all the others.

But who are all the others?
Adolescents who are just
Beginning to embark on
A journey of a lifetime.

He talks and I listen.
His eyes tell a story
Of sadness and despair,
Of love and compassion.

He is alone in his world.
He has chosen to survive
A life filled with turmoil and
Chaos, one day at a time.

He has great goals and dreams.
No doubt he will succeed.
His strong passion for life
Looks to tomorrow.

These words are written for him,
Hoping that he never gives up.
He is an incredible
Young man, unlike all the others!

My Afterthoughts

Date:

_____
_____
_____
_____
_____
_____
_____
_____
_____
_____
_____
_____
_____
_____
_____
_____
_____
_____

It Makes Me Sad

Someone knocks on my door. An extremely artistic young girl looks at me with big green eyes and a warm smile. Almost a year has gone by since we last spoke. She continues to fight her addiction with drugs one day at a time. Her voice sounds stronger. Why then, as I write these words, does my heart feel so heavy?

It makes me sad that you
can't look at me,
so fearful of seeing
what lies inside.

What makes you think that I
have a right to
judge you as a person?
We are equal.

Please look in the mirror.
You are the judge.
You are the jury now
and forever.

Forgiveness heals the soul.
Look within and
find what makes you happy
and brings you peace.

Living one day at a
time has become
a way of life so that
you *will* survive!

My Afterthoughts

Date: _____

_____
_____
_____
_____
_____
_____
_____
_____
_____
_____
_____
_____
_____
_____
_____
_____
_____

It's Time to Turn the Brain On

Everyone has a right to fail ... but does everyone want to?

Remorseful words sound so sincere.
Failure triggers disappointment.
Basketball creates excitement.
What is stopping him from passing?

"Respectful and capable"
is what all the teachers say.
Is failing cool, or is it
a habit; who really knows?

There is no logic, nor is there
a reasonable answer to
this most agitating pattern,
a most discouraging downfall.

I relate learning to eating,
both essential to survive.
What is his favorite meal?
Chicken and rice, so he says.

If all the right ingredients
are put into a pot, and he
forgets to turn the stove on, what
will happen to his luscious meal?

It will be destroyed, just like
his brain is being wasted.
He is smart, and he has goals,
goals that are attainable.

Now is the time to turn the brain
on; now is the time to focus
on taking control of his life.
Now is the time to start doing!

My Afterthoughts

Date: _____

_____

_____

_____

_____

_____

_____

_____

_____

_____

_____

_____

_____

_____

_____

_____

_____

Awaken

Every few months, this soft-spoken, blue-eyed adolescent would stop by my office to talk. Who he was during his high school years and who he is today are two different people. Those chaotic years are long gone, yet the guilt and shame are holding him hostage. Forgiveness is the key to his awakening.

From the outside:
eyes of blue,
a tender smile,
a warm heart.

From the inside:
confusion,
a tornado
swirling through.

Peel the layers:
one, two, three.
Slowly, gently,
search within.

Show me, lead me,
find my soul.
Tears fall lightly.
Forgive me.

My Afterthoughts

Date: _____

_____
_____
_____
_____
_____
_____
_____
_____
_____
_____
_____
_____
_____
_____
_____
_____
_____
_____

There Is Always Hope

Where there is darkness … there is light

Sun gives us light
Rain gives us hope
Hope is the water
That runs through our veins
And allows us to live
just when we are ready to
give up!

My Afterthoughts

Date: _____

_____

_____

_____

_____

_____

_____

_____

_____

_____

_____

_____

_____

_____

_____

_____

_____

Day Three ... Alone

These words are for every teenager who is in the midst of a break-up. Love hurts. Today is day three of heartache.

Eyes tired,
Tired of crying,
A heavy heart.

Was it love?
I thought it was love.
No, it *was* love.

We are young.
Allow time to heal:
Words of wisdom.

I hear them
I do not feel them.
It hurts so badly.

What was it?
It was different.
I believed.

Emptiness,
I am so confused.
Day three ... alone.

My Afterthoughts

Date: _____

_____

_____

_____

_____

_____

_____

_____

_____

_____

_____

_____

_____

_____

_____

_____

_____

Fly Away Into Freedom

Years have passed and this beautiful young girl remains a prisoner. She is being held captive by an abusive relationship. The time has come to let go. Is she ready?

She speaks
softly,
sincerely.

Eyes well.
Tears flow.
Emotions stir.

Hurt
Anger
Fear

Young love, poisoned.
Young love turned into
power and possession.

She trusted.
She believed.
She was blinded.

Years have gone by.

An aching heart
continues to weigh heavily
on her soul.

The engines roar.
It's time to let go.
Hold steady.

Fly away
slowly through the clouds.
Freedom awaits!

My Afterthoughts

Date: _____

_____

_____

_____

_____

_____

_____

_____

_____

_____

_____

_____

_____

_____

_____

_____

_____

_____

Speak Quickly

Never before had this young girl approached my office. It was the first time she ever opened up. Her words came spewing out at one hundred miles an hour. Her tears began to fall. Within a few moments, she came to a stop. Here is her story of friendship gone astray.

Speak quickly …

Years of thoughts were traveling through her head. What happened? She lost her best friend. She lost her boyfriend to her best friend. What is a friend? She trusted her. Why? What makes someone change? Is it the drugs? Do they play with your mind? Do they make you not care? Do they ruin a friendship? Did the drugs replace their friendship? What makes *her* not use? She could, but she chooses not to.

Senior year was supposed to be the fun year. It's turned into a nightmare. Why does she care so much? What is her role in life? Who is she? She is smart. She is pretty. She has a great future ahead of her. Does she know that she is smart? Yes. Does she know that she is pretty? I don't think so. Does she know that she has a great future ahead of her? Absolutely. Does she know that she has the power of choice? She learned that lesson today. Why is she so sad? It's easy … the rules of the friendship have changed. She was always the one who protected her friend. She was always the one who helped her friend if she needed help in class. She was always the one who forgave the unforgivable. She was even willing to forgive her friend for stealing her boyfriend. Yet her friend won't speak to her! Her friend doesn't need her today. What did she do wrong? Absolutely nothing! She is the caregiver. She protects. She is seeking approval.

It's time to stop. Look in the mirror and see the person who needs her right now. She is a beautiful young girl with big blue eyes. She is the person who loves her family. She is the person who has always pleased her parents. She is the person who is tired of pleasing her parents. She is the person who is in competition with her sister. She is the person who is tired of competing. She is the person who is extremely smart. She is the person who knows right from wrong. She is the person who has tried so hard to be good. She is the person who has followed the right path. She is the person who is afraid to let go of a friendship. She is the person who is scared of being lonely. She is the person who is growing up. She is the person who is learning life's greatest lesson … love thyself.

My Afterthoughts

Date: _____

_____
_____
_____
_____
_____
_____
_____
_____
_____
_____
_____
_____
_____
_____
_____
_____
_____
_____

Look In The Mirror … What Do I See?

This very confused fourteen-year-old is angry that her parents' divorce has created a life of turmoil.

a tender young girl

a tender young girl with sullen green eyes

a beautiful, tender young girl with long flowing brown hair

a smart, beautiful, tender young girl whose heart is full of sorrow

an angry, smart, beautiful, tender young girl whose future is in jeopardy

she screams.

she shakes.

she accuses.

she blames.

she cries.

"Why?"

My Afterthoughts

Date: _____

_____
_____
_____
_____
_____
_____
_____
_____
_____
_____
_____
_____
_____
_____
_____
_____
_____

I Just Want To Be Happy

A young blonde blue-eyed girl walks into my office, sits down, and begins to softly cry. She looks very tired. Her girlfriend told her to speak with me. She begins to speak about the abusive relationship she is in. It's been about one year. She is not allowed to speak to anyone without his permission. She is not allowed to go anywhere without his permission. She is scared. She feels trapped. She knows it's wrong, yet she doesn't know how to get out of it.

My door opens.
There she sits,
head down,
eyes drawn.

"Sit down," I say.
Who is she?
Helpless
tears flow.

She speaks softly
and slowly,
trying
to speak

Of a love that
is deadly.
She feels
afraid.

Her phone buzzes.
Texting starts:
nasty,
cruel words.

In a meek and
solemn voice,
she cries
aloud,

"I just want to be happy."

Remember: No one has a right to hurt you ... mentally or physically. It is time to get out of this abusive relationship. You are the most important person in the whole wide world. Look in the mirror. She is the one who will look back at you forever. You are beautiful. Talk to someone who will help you ... your mother, your father, your teacher, your friends. They will be there for you. They will help you find the strength you need to get through this tough time. Trust me. It is time. Repeat this affirmation each day. "I am a beautiful human being with feelings. Today I choose to be happy!"

Date:

My Afterthoughts

_____

_____

_____

_____

_____

_____

_____

_____

_____

_____

_____

_____

_____

_____

_____

_____

_____

A Familiar Voice

In her senior year, this very sensitive and insecure teenager wanted to end her life. All she has ever wanted is for someone to love her. Her biggest fear is being left alone. The phone rings. She cries softly as she speaks of a love now gone. All she needed was to hear a familiar voice.

Amidst the chaotic confusion,
the office phone rings.
Years have passed since the dismal dark voice
on the other end
So frantically fought back thoughts
of taking her life.
She speaks softly, slowly, tearfully,
of today's breakup.
She silently suffers within her
own world of sadness.
With a tearful tone, she speaks of him
And their connection,
The indescribable innocence
they shared together.
Can she sustain the painful prison
of being alone?

My Afterthoughts

Date: _____

_____
_____
_____
_____
_____
_____
_____
_____
_____
_____
_____
_____
_____
_____
_____
_____
_____
_____

Someday You Will Find the Answers

An extremely intelligent, independent, and sensitive young girl abandoned by her mother at the age of five searches for the lost child within.

Those sad, tender, young eyes,
deep brown pools of darkness
staring into the distance;

That soft innocent voice,
looking for the answers
to life's greatest mysteries.

Who am I?
Where am I?
The lost child:

Someday
you will have answers.

Someday
you will want to trust.

Someday
you will understand.

Someday
you will give yourself

Permission
to erupt,
to explode,

Allowing your thoughts and
emotions to surface.
Emptiness and loneliness

will fade away,
and then, "Good-bye,
wall of silence."

My Afterthoughts

Date: _____

_____

_____

_____

_____

_____

_____

_____

_____

_____

_____

_____

_____

_____

_____

_____

Diagnosis … Cancer

This very sad fourteen-year-old girl wipes the tears from her eyes as she speaks of her grandfather's diagnosis. She respects his wishes. She will not go to the hospital. She will remember him as healthy … smiling … alive.

Cancer, creating chaos
within.
Deadly, darkening disease,
uninvited,
stealing, slithering sloth,
destroying.

The fight begins …

Sunshine sneaking steadily
inside,
holding hearts hopeful,
united,
living life lovingly,
surviving.

The fight goes on!

My Afterthoughts

Date:

Happily Ever After

With love in his heart and tears in his eyes, this seventeen-year-old boy finds the strength to speak to his mother about the day that changed his life forever … the day that changed his family forever … the day that has held him captive forever. It is time to let go. It is time to move on. It is time to accept the truth.

Dear Mom,

When I was only seven years old, you told me that everything was going to be okay. Then why did I feel so scared? You told me that our family would always stay together. Then why did Dad stop coming home at night? You told me, "Don't worry. I love you." Then why did you look so sad? I felt it then. It was that horrible feeling … that sad feeling … that sick feeling … that deep-in-the-gut feeling. I felt it then. Something was wrong. It was. "Help," I cried silently to myself. I tried desperately to keep that smile on my face. Ten years have passed. I am still crying on the inside. I am still smiling on the outside. You continue to tell me that everything will be okay. It isn't. You pretend that our family is still together. We aren't. You tell me that it is nobody's business. It isn't. There is nothing to be ashamed of, Mom. Our family has been torn apart. It was Dad who chose to leave. It is not my fault. It is not your fault. Everything is going to be okay. We will always be together. Don't worry, Mom, I love you. It's time to face the truth. It's time to stop pretending. It's time for acceptance. It's time to live again … happily ever after!

Love forever,
Your Son

My Afterthoughts

_____
_____
_____
_____
_____
_____
_____
_____
_____
_____
_____
_____
_____
_____
_____
_____

P.S. "and Lunch"

At the age of fifteen, this very intelligent and intimidated young girl's folder sat untouched in my file cabinet for one year. It contained her academic records. It did not speak of the emotional pain attached to those failing grades. Today her story comes alive. Today the bullying stops!

Dear _____,

      When you walked into my office on that September morning, I had no idea about who you were or the kind of hell you had gone through for the past four years. Within the first few minutes of meeting you, the person I saw was a very intelligent young girl with deep brown eyes, a beautiful smile, and an extremely sensitive and humorous personality. There was an immediate connection. I had no clue what was to come. I only knew that I felt something … something that was very special … but what was it?

      Kids are my life. Teaching is my love. When I listened to your story, I was appalled and disgusted that another human being could be so cruel! I was angered by the reaction of the adults. I could not change what happened, but I would be darned if it would continue. I remember telling you that I promised no one would hurt you at _____ High School and that I vowed you would be safe. It was at that moment that I became your *voice*.

      I have been your voice for the past fourteen months, and I will continue to be until you have the power to speak for yourself. You were just a name … a name on a folder that arrived in my office the previous September from middle school … a girl whose folder I held on to for an entire year … never knowing the reason behind her choice to switch schools … a girl who chose not to come to _____ High School as a freshman … a girl who chose to go to another school to avoid the pain and destruction that she had suffered over the past three years. I had no idea that this young girl was running away … running away from the bullies … running away from hell.

      As time went on and your mother began to unfold the nightmare that you lived during those three years in middle school, my heart began to ache. As an educator, I could not fathom how this horrific behavior was allowed. Yet staying angry is not the answer. Turning anger into awareness is the right choice. Together we can educate adults and students alike about the physical and emotional pain that these bullies instill, giving the victims the power within to stand up and fight back. I promise you your voice will be heard. No one has a right to strip you of your self-worth. No one has a right to destroy you!

Love,
Mrs. D.

P.S. "… and lunch!"

I promised her lunch if she would come and speak with me at a bullying workshop. Reluctantly, she did come with me and miraculously she found the power within to relive her nightmare. The audience gave her a standing ovation. That day changed her life forever

My Afterthoughts

_____

_____

_____

_____

_____

_____

_____

_____

_____

_____

_____

_____

_____

_____

_____

_____

Healing From the Inside Out

Sexually abused by her stepfather, this beautiful, brown-eyed fifteen-year-old girl struggles to live one day at a time.

Fifteen years old,
the world on
her shoulders.
Life isn't fair.
Expect nothing.
Get nothing.

Why so negative?

four years old ... abused

five years old ... abused

six years old ... abused

seven years old ... abused

eight years old ... abused

nine years old ... abused

ten years old ... abused

eleven years old ... abused

twelve years old ... abused

Why so angry?

Feelings numbed,
body and mind
separated
for survival.
When can healing
begin?
TODAY,
if she allows it.

My Afterthoughts

The Secret Is Out

A very humble parent shared her story with me … giving hope to any young person who is facing physical or mental abuse. No one has the right to abuse you. No one has the right to destroy you. You have the power within you to stop being abused. You are not alone. Please get the help you need. Please tell someone!

I WAS JUST A YOUNG GIRL
LOVING LIFE
WHEN YOU STOLE A PART OF ME:
MY INNOCENCE … MY YOUTH.
PLAYING YOUR GAME,
FOLLOWING YOUR RULES,
THE STAKES WERE HIGH:
LOTS OF PENNIES FOR ME,
AND, IN RETURN,
PLEASURE FOR YOU.
I REMEMBER THOSE WORDS,
"IT'S OUR SECRET."
WHO WERE YOU KIDDING?
IT WAS BLACKMAIL.
IT WAS YOUR SECRET,
YOUR SICKNESS.
A SELFISH, DISGUSTING ACT
MEANT TO GRATIFY ONLY **YOU.**
YOU … A MAN I'VE GROWN TO HATE,
A HATRED THAT HAS CONSUMED ME
FOR FORTY YEARS,
REPRESSED DEEP WITHIN
ONLY TO SURFACE TODAY.
I TRUSTED YOU.
I LOVED YOU.
I RESPECTED YOU.
YOU WERE MY FAMILY.
YOU WERE MY BLOOD,
AND NOW
YOU ARE NOTHING,
NOTHING TO ME.
THE SECRET IS OUT … I AM
THE GAME IS OVER!

Forty years have passed since she was abused by her teenage uncle … vowing to keep it a secret from her mother … choosing to keep the family intact. She never told anyone … until today … the day she buried her mother. The secret is out. She is free!

My Afterthoughts

Date: _____

_____
_____
_____
_____
_____
_____
_____
_____
_____
_____
_____
_____
_____
_____
_____
_____
_____

It Always Seems Like Yesterday

Six years after her father's death, this very soft-spoken young girl sat with a classmate whose mother had just passed away. When he told her that his mother died yesterday, she looked at him, smiled, and quietly remarked, "It always seems like yesterday."

Dying is
so final,
so real,
so sad,
Yet it always seems like yesterday.
Minutes pass,
days pass,
hours pass,
years pass,
Yet it always seems like yesterday.
Sun rises,
sun sets.
she giggles,
she cries.
Yet it always seems like yesterday.
Just ten years
old when
daddy died,
it stings.
Yet it always seems like yesterday.
Memories
of love,
sweet sixteen,
it hurts.
Yet it always seems like yesterday.
Sun rises
sun sets.
she giggles,
she cries.
Yet it always seems like yesterday.
Dying is
so final,
so real,
so sad.
I love you, daddy.

My Afterthoughts

Date: _____

_____
_____
_____
_____
_____
_____
_____
_____
_____
_____
_____
_____
_____
_____
_____
_____
_____
_____

A Letter from Pop

A year and a half has gone by since the death of his grandfather, and this extremely distraught fifteen year old boy is finding it difficult to move forward. He is angry. He is sad. He is upset that he never got to say good-bye to his grandfather. He was finally able to write a good-bye letter to Pop. It was the first time that he cried since his grandfather's death. He thanked him for teaching him about life. He thanked him for giving him a great appreciation for music and dancing. He thanked him for being the greatest role model in the world! The following is Pop's response to this precious letter:

Dear Grandson,
I received your letter today. It brought tears to my eyes. I am so proud of you. I miss you, too. I love you. Please know that I am at peace. It is time for you to find peace. Although we are apart, always remember: I am with you forever. I am a part of you. I am in your heart. I am in your soul! Letting go doesn't mean forgetting, it means remembering … remembering all of the great times we had together … remembering all of the laughter that we shared … remembering all of the memories that we created. Love lives on. Love never ends. Below is a poem I wrote just for you. Keep it in my socks that you tucked away in your drawer the day I left you. Remember these words forever, especially when you are dancing!

*I see the smile on your face
each time you speak my name.*

*I taste the tears that flow from your eyes
each time you speak my name.*

*I hear the love in your voice
each time you speak my name.*

*I feel the weight of your soul
each time you speak my name.*

*The time has come to let me go
So I can rest in peace.*

*The time has come to let me go
So you can live again.*

*Don't be afraid;
I am with you forever.
I love you!*

Love,
Pop

Date:

My Afterthoughts

Life Goes On

Today she buried her father ... feelings of sadness ... heartache within ... a beautiful ceremony ... an honorable tribute to a well-respected man.

Sitting in the park with sunlight on her back,
cars slowly meandering around each turn,
people walking, riding bikes, and playing ball,
a gentle wind blows the sweet smells of summer.

A train quickly comes and goes in an instant;
just like life, it, too, hurries on by.
In a split second he was taken away.
In a split second her world became silent.

Who remains after death: family and friends?
Pictures, laughter, tears, and stories of the past?
Time moves on, and the hot sun begins to set.
Warm memories are stored in her mind ... life goes on.

Date: _____

My Afterthoughts

_____
_____
_____
_____
_____
_____
_____
_____
_____
_____
_____
_____
_____
_____
_____
_____
_____
_____
_____

A Synopsis of Life Using Drugs

If life with drugs mirrors life without drugs, what's the big deal? What's wrong with drinking and using drugs? Speak to an adolescent who has lived his/her high school years using drugs. Speak to the parents of that high school student who made the choice to use drugs. Their stories are all the same. They all live the same nightmare. The characters change. The plot remains the same. The ending is always unknown! Please read the following poem if you are thinking of experimenting with drugs. I wrote it several years ago when I counseled with one of my students who chose to use drugs. Years have gone by, and each time I am faced with counseling a young person who is caught up in the drug world, I find myself repeating the same words over and over and over again.

no feelings … no emotions
no family … no real friends
no money
no *me*
just drugs
good versus evil
darkness … deceit … danger
inner turmoil
struggling
scared
lonely
where am I?
life
death
choices
who am I?

My Afterthoughts

Date: _____

_____
_____
_____
_____
_____
_____
_____
_____
_____
_____
_____
_____
_____
_____
_____
_____
_____
_____

Trust Happens If You Allow It

It is her first day back from a five-day suspension. She tested positive for marijuana. She is angry with the person who snitched on her. She blames that person for ruining her life. She cries. She is scared. She started using in eighth grade ... a lifestyle that has continued over the past four years. And now it has come to an abrupt halt. What does she do now? All of her friends are using. What will she do after school? How will she fit in? She wants to use. It makes her feel good, but she is scared. She knows the consequences. She looks at the clock. The time is moving so slowly. She shakes her head. Will she survive? She despises counseling. She has tried it before ... last year ... when someone noticed the cuts on her arms. It's funny. Someone cares more about her than she cares about herself. What is she running away from? It's time to stop blaming and start feeling.

I know it hurts.
I can tell by the look in your eyes.
I can hear by the sound of your voice.
I can see by the tears on your cheek.

You look at me,
Searching for the answers.
I look at you,
Hoping to find answers.

You are angry,
Blaming everyone else.
Why get tested
When you were not using?

Dirty urine:
Five days clean, and now what?
Those dreaded words,
"You must get counseling."

Having to trust
Someone enough to share
Those gut feelings?
NO WAY ... then why trust me?

You allowed it
To happen ... a stranger
Earned your trust.
The time has come

To grow up and
Confront those deep feelings
Without drugs.
The battle has begun.

My Afterthoughts

Date:

_____
_____
_____
_____
_____
_____
_____
_____
_____
_____
_____
_____
_____
_____
_____
_____
_____
_____

From Someone Who Cares

Trying to fool everyone, this very sensitive and talented young man has found himself addicted to drugs. He started with drinking, moved to marijuana, and now cocaine has become his drug of choice. He is lost. He needs help. He is in denial. Below is a letter I wrote to him after hours and hours of counseling.

Dear_____,

Drugs are a killer. They steal away the person you are. They steal away the life in you. They steal away your future. They steal away your smile. They steal away your beautiful blue eyes. They steal away your every breath. I don't believe you really want to use drugs. I don't believe you feel you belong in the world of darkness. I don't believe you deserve to live in the world of fear ... fear of death ... fear of being locked up. I don't believe you want to be a druggie.

For two years I've watched an angry, angry, angry young boy turn into a very caring young man. Remember, at age fifteen, you made the choice. You told me that you were ready to change and that you wanted counseling. You did it. You were proud of yourself and you should be. I am proud of you, too. You became the person you are today. And now ... at age seventeen ... you are faced with another challenge. This one is even tougher than the death of grandpa. This one is your very own death — the death of your soul. Drugs are taking the life out of you. They are killing you slowly ... one day at a time. It makes me sick to watch, but I know that you can stop it ... if you want to. You can stop using. The choice is yours.

Remember, you have made it to where you are today because you wanted to change. I am asking you a question only you can answer. "Do you want to keep using?" If you do, you know the consequences. We have done everything possible to help you understand the world of drugs. We've given you all the resources to help you stop using. We have talked until we're blue in the face. The talking is over! Your parents are now involved. The school is involved, and the bottom line is, who really cares?

You will do exactly what you want to do. You will live your life however you see fit. When no one is watching, the only person you have to face is yourself. You go to sleep with yourself. You wake up with yourself. You have to look at yourself in the mirror. You only have to answer to yourself. I know you have a conscience. I know that you are really a very sensitive human being. I know that you are in turmoil. If you allow yourself to face the truth, you will start to live again. Maybe I am nuts, but I believe in you. Just seven days ago, I was so angry with you, and today my heart aches for you. You see, the people who have raised you live an addicted life, too. It is a roller coaster ride of emotions ... up and down. Anger, sadness, and confusion! There's nothing else to say right now. I pray for you. I pray you get the strength to do what you need to do. I pray you will someday see the person I see. I pray for you ... one day at a time.

Love,
Mrs. D.

P.S. Grandpa is praying for you, too!

Date:

My Afterthoughts

To A Young Girl from an Adult

It has only been one week since this very confused seventeen-year-old track star found her way into my office. Her last few months had been consumed with lies and deceit. She is feeling guilty and shameful for what she has done, yet she is chooses to continue down a destructive path. Tearfully, she questioned, "Why is this is happening to me?" Her words were so deep that I could see the windows of her soul. The following poem portrays the life of this extremely talented and intelligent adolescent whose world had been invaded by drugs and deception.

young
pretty
confused
feels angry
trusts no one
running scared
abusing drugs
ridden with guilt
thinks negatively
used to be happy
afraid of knowing self
displays risky behaviors
choosing a path of destruction
wasting talent and intelligence

bored
alone
hurting
lost spirit
feels empty
questions why
fooling herself
suffers heartache
living a nightmare
making poor choices
denies having problem
blinded by consequences
compromising value system
creating havoc at home and school

Date:

My Afterthoughts

scared
lonely
worried
lost her soul
fears unknown
wants freedom
hides behind mask
parties with friends
disgusted with lies
looking for way out
crying on the inside
exploding on the outside
pretending to be someone else
tormented by the world of darkness

real
aching
destroyed
seeking self
loves parents
taught respect
filled with beauty
lost sight of goals
raised with honesty
looking for answers
searching for happiness
ready to explore the world
surviving one day at a time
afraid to stop and smell the roses

She is scared. She feels trapped. She wants help. These words are for every young girl who thinks she is fooling everyone.
If you are caught up in this dark place, please find someone you trust and get the help you need. It's time to stop and
smell the roses.

My Afterthoughts

Date:

64

Life Is Precious

One day a very distraught seventeen-year-old girl walked into my office ... a girl who frequently sat with me throughout the past year, but this time it was different.

She sat down and began to babble on and on about how unfair life was. She repeated the same questions she had asked several times before. How could a mother stop being a mother? How could a child be expected to raise herself at the age of twelve? Being brought up by addicted parents created the turbulent world she lived in—a world consumed with alcohol and drugs. She had been the pawn for cocaine at the age of three, and now, fourteen years later, she was a senior in high school. She had chosen to follow in her parents' footsteps, experimenting with several drugs starting at the age of thirteen. She, too, was addicted, but today she was tired. She was ready to give up. She looked at me. With tears rolling down her cheeks, she asked, "Why should I keep going on? What's the purpose of living?"

At that moment, I can remember feeling so inadequate. What answers do I have? I, too, am only a human being. I, too, am struggling each day to understand what my purpose is here on earth. (Don't you question your reason for existence?) It was on that cool, brisk day that I found my reason for being: to show this lost child just how unique she was, to help her see the beauty she possessed inside, and to find the right words that would give her hope. That afternoon, as I stood in Barnes & Noble bookstore, looking through several books that had been written in response to this profound question, I found the perfect book called *The Precious Present* by Spencer Johnson.

The next day, as she and I sat together in those same chairs, I read aloud the powerful words of *The Precious Present* to her. With each turning page, a tear would fall from her eyes. Those reflective words touched her soul (and mine). Even though she was asking someone who had never used a drug in her life, someone who had grown up in a world completely opposite hers, she trusted me to give her a reason for living. On that day a very special bond began to form between us: a bond that has continued throughout the years, a bond that remains as precious as the words spoken in *The Precious Present*. Since that day, there have been several other teens who have questioned the meaning of life, teens who are feeling empty inside, teens who are searching for hope. I continue to read aloud *The Precious Present*, giving each one of them the will to believe, the strength to survive, and a reason for living ... one day at a time.

(The following are quotes from several students who have defined the meaning of life. I thought you would enjoy their words of wisdom!)

"Life is like one big pimple ... oozing out"
"Life is two soft tacos and a nacho supreme."
"Life is beautiful ... whether or not you see it now!"
"Life is what YOU make of it!"
"Life is beautiful when you SPEAK!"
"Life is a struggle from beginning to end!"

My Afterthoughts

Date:

_____

_____

_____

_____

_____

_____

_____

_____

_____

_____

_____

_____

_____

_____

_____

_____

A Second Chance

Seven days have passed since the phone rang last Friday morning. A young girl cried hysterically as she told me that her boyfriend had been rushed to the hospital. He took some pills. He may have to go on life support. She asked me if I knew why. Why would the boy she loves try to end his life? Only he knows why, and today he has a second chance to live and to answer the question why.

One week ago …

overdose

Oxygen
Sleep
Stillness

Today

Breathing
Awake
Movement

life

One week ago …

overdose

Darkness
Silence
Tears

Today …

Light
Truth
Hope

life

a second chance … to live!

My Afterthoughts

Date:

_____

_____

_____

_____

_____

_____

_____

_____

_____

_____

_____

_____

_____

_____

_____

_____

_____

Dreams Do Come True ... If Only You Believe

For years this beautiful and talented seventeen-year-old girl blamed her mother for the life she was living. When does the blame stop? When does she start living?

Dear_____,

Although I have only known you for a short while, I see a young girl who is living in fear and afraid of the unknown, afraid of making mistakes, afraid of what tomorrow will bring, afraid of being happy, afraid of liking herself, afraid of letting go of old habits, afraid of life without using, afraid of looking at herself in the mirror, afraid of seeing her real self, afraid of succeeding, afraid of life.

There is not one answer, but there are choices ... *forever* ... choices ... decisions ... more choices and more decisions. No one ever knows if she is making the right decision; you can only follow your heart and do what is right for you at the moment. You know what you need to do. You know that you don't like your life where it is right now. You know that you are headed in the wrong direction. Believe it or not, you are in control of your life. The choice is yours ... good or evil. It is all up to you. That is the scary part. There is no one else to blame but yourself. Life was much simpler when you were younger and you could blame your mother for your mistakes, but now you are grown up, and the only person you can blame is yourself.

Think about what you want for yourself. Do you want to be successful? Do you want to be able to look at yourself in the mirror and like what you see? Do you want to look into those big green eyes and see what I see? You are a beautiful young girl with an enormous amount of talent. You have the intelligence to do whatever you set your mind to. You need to believe that you have the power within to be whatever you choose to be. You need to learn to love yourself, and you need to stop using so that your mind can clear and you can think straight. No one can do it for you.

I believe in you. I also believe in the power of prayer. The choice is yours. You deserve the best because you are the best. You are a very extraordinary person. Thank you for trusting me. I pray that you find the strength within to make the right decision. Always remember ... live life one day at a time. Dreams do come true ... if only you believe!

Love,
Mrs. D.

My Afterthoughts

Date:

_____

_____

_____

_____

_____

_____

_____

_____

_____

_____

_____

_____

_____

_____

_____

_____

_____

The World of Drugs vs. The World of Sports

While counseling with an extremely talented athlete who was experimenting with drugs, I found myself relating the world of drugs to the world of sports. Presenting the facts became more powerful than attempting to persuade him to stop using. The following few pages simply compare the world of drugs to the world of sports. The first two collages I've created represent these two separate worlds ... the world of darkness and the world of light ... good versus evil! The third collage symbolizes the two worlds combined. They are followed by my synopsis of what life may be using drugs versus what life can be without using drugs. Remember ... you are in control of your life ... you live ... you die. The way you choose to live your life is your choice. Which picture do you relate to? What world do you belong in?

Scene 1...The World of Drugs   Scene 2...The World of Sports

Scene 3...Two Worlds Combined

My Afterthoughts

Date:

_____
_____
_____
_____
_____
_____
_____
_____
_____
_____
_____
_____
_____
_____
_____
_____
_____
_____
_____

Scene 1...The World of Drugs

My Afterthoughts

Date: _____

_____

_____

_____

_____

_____

_____

_____

_____

_____

_____

_____

_____

_____

_____

_____

_____

You and Drugs ... Just the Facts:
No emotions, no feelings, no family involved.

Drugging is not a spectator's sport. Family is not invited to watch you use. There are no fans to cheer. There are no winners. There is no competition. The scoreboard always remains the same 0 – 0.

Life Using Drugs

- You *can* go to high school ... *if you are using* ... you may be drug tested ... suspension.
- You *can* play sports ... *if you are using* ... you may be drug tested ... suspension.
- You *can* graduate ... *if you are using* ... your grades suffer ... discipline problems occur.
- You *can* get your license ... *if you are using* ... you are risking your life and others' ... you may face jail time.
- You *can* go on to college ... *if you are using* ... you are risking your chances of graduating.
- You *can* play sports ... *if you are using* ... you may be drug tested ... expulsion.
- You *can* get a job ... *if you are using* ... you may be drug tested ... you will be fired.
- You *can* have a relationship ... *if you are using* ... the road will be rocky.
- You *can* have friends ... *if you are using* ... chances are your "*friends*" will be using, too.
- You *can* get married ... *if you are using* ... will your spouse be using too?
- You *can* have a home ... *if you are using* ... will your home be the drug haven?
- You *can* have children ... *if you are using* ... you *will* lead by example.
- You *can* go on vacation ... *if you are using* ... chances are there will be no money left to spend on vacation.
- You *can* continue working ... *if you are using* ... chances are you have used a lot of your sick time.
- You *can* have grandchildren ... *if you are using* ... you *will* continue to lead by example.
- You *can* retire ... *if you are using* ... chances are your quality of life will be affected.
- You *will* die ... *if you are using* ... who will be with you at death?

My Afterthoughts

Date: _____

_____
_____
_____
_____
_____
_____
_____
_____
_____
_____
_____
_____
_____
_____
_____
_____
_____

Scene 2 ... The World of Sports

Scene 2...The World of Sports

My Afterthoughts

Date:

You and Sports … Just the Facts
Emotions, feelings, and families involved

Football, baseball, basketball, wrestling, hockey, golf, tennis, bowling, and cheerleading are all spectator sports. Family is invited to watch you play. There are plenty of excited fans to cheer you on. There are always winners/losers. The scoreboard represents real competition.

Life without using drugs

- You *can* go to high school … *if you are not using* … no drug test … keep learning!
- You *can* play sports … *if you are not using* … no drug test … keep playing!
- You *can* graduate … *if you are not using* … you can graduate … drug free!
- You *can* get a license … *if you are not using* … you will have more control behind the wheel!
- You *can* go to college … *if you are not using* … no drug test … keep learning!
- You *can* play sports … *if you are not using* …no drug test … keep playing!
- You *can* get a job … *if you are not using* … no drug test … keep working!
- You *can* have a relationship … *if you are not using* … your mind will be clear to make the right decisions!
- You *can* have friends … *if you are not using* … chances are your *"friends"* will not be using either!
- You *can* get married … *if you are not using* … chances are your spouse will be drug free!
- You *can* have a home … *if you are not using* … your home will be drug free!
- You *can* have children … *if you are not using* … you *will* lead by example!
- You *can* go on vacation … *if you are not using* … you will have some extra spending money!
- You *can* have grandchildren … *if you are not using* …you *will* lead by example!
- You *can* continue working …*if you are not using* … no drug test … keep working!
- You *can* retire … *if you are not using* … enjoy life…drug free!
- You *can* live … *if you are not using* … you will have the love and support of your family!
- You *will* die … *if you are not using* … you will have the love and support of your family!

My Afterthoughts

Date: _____

_____

_____

_____

_____

_____

_____

_____

_____

_____

_____

_____

_____

_____

_____

_____

_____

_____

_____

Scene 3 ... Two Worlds Combined

Scene 3...Two Worlds Combined

My Afterthoughts

_____
_____
_____
_____
_____
_____
_____
_____
_____
_____
_____
_____
_____
_____
_____
_____
_____

Two Worlds Combined

Look on the previous page for this talented track star as he runs past his dark world. How did he get involved in drugs? What happened? Why has he chosen to go against all he believes in? He is searching for answers. Since you are his best friend, maybe you can give him some insight into the choices he has made. Below are a few important facts to help you write a personal letter to your friend. Please be honest. He is feeling desperate!

- The main character is a very popular high school athlete who is fighting *the most* difficult battle of his life. He started using drugs in junior year. Marijuana is his drug of choice. He has tried cocaine and ecstasy. No one knows. It is his secret!

- You have been best friends for four years. He has pushed you away. He is hanging out with another group. You know he is using.

- He is a valuable member of the track team and soccer team. He says that he wants to quit.

- He ranks in the top twenty percent of his graduating class, but his grades are dropping.

- He is well liked by his coaches and teachers. They see a drastic change in his behavior.

- He loves his family. They love him, but they are constantly fighting.

- His family has gone to all his games since he started playing sports. They always cheer him on.

- His family is proud of him. They have no idea he has a drug problem.

- Where does he go when no one is watching?

- He is torn between two worlds … good versus evil!

My Afterthoughts

Date: _____

_____

_____

_____

_____

_____

_____

_____

_____

_____

_____

_____

_____

_____

_____

_____

_____

_____

_____

A Letter To My Friend ... Because I Care

*Dear*_____,

_____

_____

_____

_____

_____

_____

_____

_____

_____

_____

_____

_____

_____

_____

_____

_____

_____

_____

_____

_____

_____

_____

_____

_____

_____

_____

_____

_____

_____

_____

_____

_____

_____

_____

_____

_____

_____

_____

_____

My Afterthoughts

Date: _____

_____
_____
_____
_____
_____
_____
_____
_____
_____
_____
_____
_____
_____
_____
_____
_____
_____

To Those Parents/Guardians Who Are Guilty ...
Guilty of loving their children

Time and time again I've repeated the same words to the parent/guardian of an adolescent whose life has been turned upside down.

It doesn't matter what the situation is or the degree of severity; I hear the same questions over and over and over. There is confusion, embarrassment, and disappointment from both the child and the adult. Each one is searching for answers. Each one is searching for the right words to say. Each one is scared of the unknown. As a parent/guardian, feelings of guilt become overwhelming. Why? How didn't I know? Where did I go wrong? I sure have been fooled. I trusted my child. He/she knows right from wrong! My answer is always the same. You *are* guilty ... guilty of loving your child. If you didn't love, you wouldn't feel the way you do today! The time has come to face the truth and get the help that is needed.

My Afterthoughts

Date: _____

_____
_____
_____
_____
_____
_____
_____
_____
_____
_____
_____
_____
_____
_____
_____
_____
_____
_____

The Adolescent Mind … As Seen By An Adult

After counseling with hundreds of adolescents, I've created the following collage that depicts their tumultuous thoughts.

My Afterthoughts

Date:

Confused People

One sunny spring afternoon I received a note in my mailbox from a very special young girl. It read, "Hi, Mrs. D. I need to talk to you about my Pre-Calculus grade. I need some guidance so call me down when you have a minute, please."

Within moments, she and her two friends appeared at my door. We talked about the level of difficulty of the class. We talked about solutions to her problem. We talked about getting extra help. We talked about the consequences of receiving a low grade. We talked about how lousy she felt. We talked about how her parents viewed the situation. With sadness in her voice, she told me that her car had been taken away because she got a C in Pre-Calculus. Very innocently she said with a snicker, "Parents are confused people." If she always receives good grades and is a good student and never gets into trouble, why did her parents punish her? She was already punishing herself. Why did they have to punish her too? She was confused about the way they were thinking.

My Afterthoughts

Date: _____

_____

_____

_____

_____

_____

_____

_____

_____

_____

_____

_____

_____

_____

_____

_____

_____

_____

The Tunnel of Love

The following is in response to Parents Are Confused People. Time moves on as parents/guardians and adolescents travel together through the tunnel of love. A tunnel that seems neverending … a tunnel filled with great emotion … a tunnel whose destination is unknown.

Parent is an adult. Adolescent is a child.
Parent has a personality. Adolescent has a personality.
Parent has hopes and dreams. Adolescent has hopes and dreams.
Parent has taught the child right from wrong. Adolescent knows right from wrong.
Parent has given the child values and beliefs. Adolescent has acquired values and beliefs.
Parent is in control of the child. Adolescent is fighting for control of the child.
Parent becomes scared of losing the child. Adolescent is ready to lose the child.
Parent cries … smiles … laughs. Adolescent … cries … smiles … laughs.
Parent loves the child. Adolescent loves the parent.
Parent and adolescent are in the midst of a power struggle.
Time moves on.
Parent has fears. Adolescent has fears.
Parent has opinions. Adolescent has opinions.
Parent wants respect. Adolescent wants respect.
Parent makes choices. Adolescent makes choices.
Parent has wants and needs. Adolescent has wants and needs.
Parent has hopes and dreams. Adolescent has hopes and dreams.
Parent is always the parent. Adolescent is always the child.
Parent cries … smiles … laughs. Adolescent … cries … smiles … laughs.
Parent loves the child. Adolescent loves the parent.
Parent and adolescent continue power struggle.
Time moves on.
Parent is scared of independence. Adolescent strives for independence.
Parent allows the child to let go. Adolescent senses the child letting go.
Parent watches the child mature. Adolescent feels the child mature.
Parent searches for happiness. Adolescent searches for happiness.
Parent has hopes and dreams. Adolescent has hopes and dreams.
Parent is an adult. Adolescent is becoming an adult.
Parent is always the parent. Adolescent is always the child.
Parent cries … smiles … laughs. Adolescent cries … smiles … laughs.
Parent loves the child. Adolescent loves the parent.
Parent and adolescent end power struggle.
Time moves on.

My Afterthoughts

Date:

_____
_____
_____
_____
_____
_____
_____
_____
_____
_____
_____
_____
_____
_____
_____
_____
_____

I Love You, My Child

Below is a poem written to every parent/guardian who has faced the greatest responsibility in life … raising a child … a child who comes with no directions … no manual … just unconditional love!

I began the role of parent with my own expectations,
my own wants and needs, my own fears and worries.

I have raised you with strong morals and beliefs.
I have taught you right from wrong.

I have but three wishes for you:
independence, health, and happiness.

I know that communication is crucial
to our existence during these difficult years.

I promise to listen to you, and in return,
I ask you to please listen to me.

As we face adolescence together
always remember …

I am your parent. I love you, my child.
I will remain in control even when you have lost control.

I am your parent. I love you, my child.
I will stick to my values and beliefs even when you have forgotten what you believe in.

I am your parent. I love you, my child.
I will listen to my inner voice even when your inner voice is silenced.

I am your parent. I love you, my child.
I will keep the door open even when you slam the door shut.

I am your parent. I love you, my child,
I will continue to believe in you even when you no longer believe in yourself.

And as adolescence ends, may these three wishes come true:
independence, health, and happiness.

I am your parent.
I love you my child … forever!

My Afterthoughts

Date:

_____
_____
_____
_____
_____
_____
_____
_____
_____
_____
_____
_____
_____
_____
_____
_____

A Letter to My Child

*Dear*_____,

_____

_____

_____

_____

_____

_____

_____

_____

_____

_____

_____

_____

_____

_____

_____

_____

_____

_____

_____

_____

_____

_____

_____

_____

_____

_____

_____

_____

_____

_____

_____

My Afterthoughts

To My Parent/Guardian

The next two poems speak to the parents/guardians of adolescents. It doesn't matter what age, sex, ethnicity or religion, every teenager has very similar thoughts and feelings. Please listen to their words.

I have my own beliefs.
I have my own values.
I have my own ideas.
I have my own feelings.

I will make my own choices.
I will make my own mistakes.
I will fall down on my own.
I will get up on my own.

I am a part of you.
I am a part of me.
I am thankful for you.
I am thankful for me.

My Afterthoughts

_____
_____
_____
_____
_____
_____
_____
_____
_____
_____
_____
_____
_____
_____
_____
_____

Let Me Fly Alone … for a while

Adolescence is a time of letting go and becoming independent.

You've given me the power to choose.
You've given me the wisdom to grow.
You've given me wings to fly.
And now the time has come
For me to break free.
Don't be scared.
You are always with me.
I will be okay.

Please,
Let me fly alone for a while,
Into the unknown,
To ask my own questions.

Please,
Let me fly alone for a while,
Into the unknown,
To find my own answers.

Please,
Let me fly alone for a while,
Into the unknown,
To make my own mistakes.

Please,
Let me fly alone for a while,
Into the unknown,
To discover who I am.

And when it's time for me to
come back home,
Let me thank you for believing in me
And trusting me to fly alone
for just a while.
I love you!

My Afterthoughts

Date: _____

_____

_____

_____

_____

_____

_____

_____

_____

_____

_____

_____

_____

_____

_____

_____

_____

_____

A Letter to My Parent/Guardian

*Dear*_____,

_____

_____

_____

_____

_____

_____

_____

_____

_____

_____

_____

_____

_____

_____

_____

_____

_____

_____

_____

_____

_____

_____

_____

_____

_____

_____

_____

_____

_____

_____

_____

_____

_____

_____

_____

_____

_____

_____

_____

_____

Date:

My Afterthoughts

Introspection

Introspection depicts life … from birth to present. The pictures below remind you of where you began and where you are going. Would you describe your life as a comedy, tragedy, mystery, or suspense? What have you learned from each event that has occurred in your life? How has it affected who you are today? Would you make any changes? Are you happy? Do you like yourself? Can you stop and smell the flowers? Please take the time to find out who you really are. You deserve it!

My Afterthoughts

Date: _____

_____

_____

_____

_____

_____

_____

_____

_____

_____

_____

_____

_____

_____

_____

_____

_____

_____

_____

Silent Passage

Adolescent = teenage thinker
Parents penalize adolescent for thinking
in response to conflicting thoughts and emotions.
Why?
We're not understood the way we need to be.
We can't understand our own thoughts and emotions.
Maybe we have to be penalized
to grow and mature.

Anonymous

Thank you for listening … thank you for writing … thank you for being you …

and always remember … you are the most important person in the whole wide world … you are a very special human being who is worthy of living … you have the power within you to make your own choices … you have the power within you to control your own thoughts … .you have the power within you to find your own happiness … you have the power within you to love yourself … the sun will shine tomorrow … if only you believe in you!

About the Author

Mrs. D. is a teacher and counselor who lives in New Jersey with her husband, children, and grandchildren. It was the transition from elementary teacher to high school counselor that sparked the makings of Afterthoughts. As a counselor, she quickly discovered that the written word is an extremely powerful tool for healing the soul. Mrs. D. is currently working on a survival guide for adolescents and parents/guardians titled "Tell Me a Story … about this crazy world called high school."

About the Illustrator

Tara Balboa is a twenty-five year old New Jersey–born artist. She studied fine arts at the School of Visual Arts in Manhattan, receiving her BFA upon graduation in 2007. Afterthoughts is her first published work.

Resources

Cancer Information Service: 800-422-6237

Child Help USA National Child Abuse Hotline: 800-4-A-CHILD (422.4453) or 800.2.A.CHILD (222.4453, TDD for hearing impaired)

National AIDS Hotline: 800-232-4636

National Association of Anorexia Nervosa & Associated Disorders (ANAD): 630-577-1330 (long distance)

National Domestic Violence/Child Abuse/ Sexual Abuse: 800-799-SAFE/800-799-7233/800-787-3224 TDD 800-942-6908 Spanish Speaking

National Drug Information Treatment and Referral Hotline: 800-662-HELP (4357)

National Parent Hotline: 800-840-6537

Nationwide RAINN National Rape Crisis Hotline: 800-656-4673

National Suicide Prevention Hotline: 1-800-SUICIDE/1-800-784-2433

National Youth Crisis Hotline: 800-442-HOPE (4673)

Recommended Readings

Albom, Mitch. *Have a Little Faith*. Hyperion, 2009

Andrews, Andy. *The Noticer*. Thomas Nelson, 2009

Blanco, Jodee. *Please Stop Laughing at Me*. Adams Media Corporation, 2003

Buscaglia, Leo. *Personhood*. Fawcett Columbine, 1978

Canfield, J., Hansen, M. V., Kirberger, K. *Chicken Soup for the Teenage Soul*. Health Comm., 1997

Carlson, Melody. *Diary of a Teenage Girl*. Multnomah Publishers, 2000

Carter-Scott, Cherie. *If Life is a Game, These are the Rules*. Broadway Books, 1998

Dellasega, Cheryl Ph.D. *Surviving Ophelia*. Ballantine Books, 2001

Dugard, Jaycee. *A Stolen Life*. Simon & Schuster, 2011

Ford, Amanda. *Be True to Yourself*. Conari Press, 2000

Gottlieb, Lori. *Stick Figure*. Berkley Books, 2000

Graham, Stedman. *Teens Can Make It Happen Workbook*. Fireside, 2001

Hesse, Herman. *Demian*. Perrenial Classics, 1925

Hornbacker, Marya. *Wasted…A Memoir of Anorexia and Bulimia*. Harper Perennial, 1998

Johnson, Spencer. *The Precious Present*. Bantam Doubleday Dell Publishing Group, 1992

Keel, Philipp. *All About Me*. Ballantine Books, 1998

Knapp, Caroline. *Drinking, A Love Story*. Delta, 1996

Kubler-Ross, Elisabeth. *On Death and Dying*. Touchstone Books, 1969

Kundtz, David. *Quiet Mind*. Conari Press, 2000

Levenkron, Steven. *Cutting*. W.W. Norton & Co., 1998

Maslow, Abraham. *Toward a Psychology of Being*. Wiley, John & Sons, Inc., 1999

Millman, Dan. *The Journeys of Socrates*. Harper Collins, 2005

Millman, Dan. *The Peaceful Warrior*. MJK, 1984

Nelson, Jane Ed.D. & Lott, Lynn. *Positive Discipline for Teenagers*. Prima, 2000

Omartian, Stormie. *Just Enough Light for the Step I'm On*. Harvest House, 1999

Paulus, Trina. *Hope for the Flowers*. Paulist Press, 1972

Peale, Norman Vincent. *The Power of Positive Thinking*. Fawcett Crest, 1952

Peck, M.Scott, M.D. *The Road Less Traveled*. Simon & Schuster, 1978

Pelzer, David. *The Child Called It*. Health Communications, 1995

Pipher, Mary Ph.D. *Reviving Ophelia*. Ballantine Books, 1994

Ryan, M.J. *Attitudes of Gratitudes*. MJF Books, 1999

Sanchez, Alex. *Rainbow Boys*. Simon & Schuster, 2001

Sanders, Mark D. & Sillers, Tia. *Climb*. Rutledge Hill Press, 2003

Sanders, Mark D. & Sillers, Tia. *I Hope You Dance*. Rutledge Hill Press, 2000

Seligman, Martin E.P., Ph.D. *Authentic Happiness*. Free Press, 2002

Shandler, Sara. *Ophelia Speaks*. Harper Perennial, 1999

Simmons, Rachel. *Odd Girl Out*. Harcourt Books, 2002

Simon, Lizzie. *Detour*. Atria Books, 2002

Smedes, Lewis B. *Forgive & Forget*. Harper Collins, 1984

Stepanek, Mattie J. T. *Reflections of a Peacemaker*. Andrews McMeel, 2005

Twerski, Abraham. *Addictive thinking … Understanding Self-Deception*. Hazelden,1997

Urban, Hal. *Life's Greatest Lessons*. Simon & Schuster Trade, 2002

Walls, Jeannette. *The Glass Castle*. Simon & Schuster Trade, 2006

Worthen, Mary. *Journey Not Chosen … Destination Not Known*. August House, 2001 adolescence, anxiety, death, divorce, drugs, fear, future, hope, illness, love, parents, relationships, respect, self, suicide, abuse, academics, addiction,

Afterthoughts

written with love...
by Mrs. D.